What am I?

1 2 3 4 5 6 7 8 9 10 Printing/Year 96 95 94 93

© 1993 Scripture Union. All rights reserved.
Published in the United States by Victor Books/
SP Publications, Inc., Wheaton, Illinois.
Printed in Singapore.

ISBN: 1-56476-148-7

What am I?

Rose Williams

Illustrations by Fred Apps

VICTOR BOOKS

A DIVISION OF SCRIPTURE PRESS PUBLICATIONS INC.
USA CANADA ENGLAND

I am fat and heavy and I'm slow
But I am very strong, you know.
God made a long thin nose for me,
To pick my dinner off a tree.
What am I?

My strong back legs are all I need
To jump along at such a speed.
God made a pocket on my tummy
So baby rides along with mummy.
What am I?

I like to live in someone's house
And play the game of chase-a-mouse.
To keep me warm God gave me fur,
And when I'm stroked I like to purr.
What am I?

God made a shell where I can hide,
And pull my arms and legs inside.
I'm very slow, as you can see,
Because I take it round with me.
What am I?

I am a tortoise, as you see,
Made specially by God to be
The only tortoise just like me.

I have a voice to sing God's praise,
A heart to love him all my days,
Two hands to clap, two eyes to see,
And ears to hear that he loves me.
What am I?

I am a person, as you see,
Made specially by God to be
The only person just like me.